SCARVES
TWO WAYS

SCARVES TWO WAYS

ISBN 13 (print): 978-1-937513-91-7
First edition

Published by Cooperative Press
http://www.cooperativepress.com

Patterns, text and charts ©2019 Andi Smith
Photos ©2019 Shannon Okey

Every effort has been made to ensure that all the information in this book is accurate at the time of publication; however, Cooperative Press neither endorses nor guarantees the content of external links referenced in this book.

If you have questions or comments about this book, or need information about licensing, custom editions, special sales, or academic/corporate purchases, please contact Cooperative Press: info@cooperativepress.com or 10252 Berea Rd, Cleveland, Ohio 44102 USA

No part of this book may be reproduced in any form, except brief excerpts for the purpose of review, without prior written permission of the publisher. Thank you for respecting our copyright.

FOR COOPERATIVE PRESS

Senior Editor: Shannon Okey
Technical Editor: Lily Anderson

SCARVES TWO WAYS

COOPERATIVE PRESS

Cleveland, Ohio

PATTERNS

Dear Prudence, page 10

Hong Kong Garden, page 14

Peek-A-Boo, page 18

Dizzy, page 22

Happy House, page 26

Arabian Nights, page 30

Kiss Them For Me, page 34

Christine, page 40

Slowdive, page 46

Spellbound, page 50

Playground Twist, page 56

Stargazer, page 62

INTRO

As most of my books seem to do, this started out as an ongoing conversation about the joys of swatching. I'd grumbled about how many times I'd match yarn to stitch pattern, only to find that I preferred a different combination, a lighter weight of yarn, a different fiber, or a completely different stitch pattern. I joked that my love of knitting scarves came from working extra long swatches - yet halfway through, I'd always wonder what the scarf looked like if I switched the DK for laceweight, or added columns of extra stitches? And thus, this book came to be.

Each of the six stitch patterns has been treated two different ways. First, as a gorgeous scarf, and then as an equally charming reimagining of the original. I chose to not take the easy option of making everything a shawl or a cowl—although many of the patterns lend themselves to that treatment—purely as a challenge to *me*, rather than for any aesthetic reason. I'd love to see all of these patterns become both cowls and shawls!

Although there are six base patterns, hopefully the different treatments I've applied to the scarves will encourage you to forget gauge, forget recommended yarn weights, and experiment with your favorite stitch patterns.

TIPS AND TRICKS

YARN CHOICE

In the Materials section of each pattern, I list the yarn I recommend, along with yardage and weight of yarn you could use to get the same results as me. However, there's no hard and fast rules when it comes to playing with scarves. If laceweight luxury is your thing, add a couple of stitch pattern repeats to get the width you want, or go bulky and take a repeat or two out. The choice is yours. Do remember though, that yardage will be different—be sure to stashdive before you cast on, or shop for enough yarn to complete your project.

NEW TO A TECHNIQUE?

Scarves are really just an extra long gauge swatch to practice and perfect those cables and wrap stitches. If you don't want to commit to diving straight into a full scarf, grab 40 or so yards of waste yarn in the weight you'll be working with, cast on the scarf, and practice new stitch patterns for a few rows to help you decide if this is the pattern for you.

CAST ON / BIND OFF

I recommend using the German Twisted cast on for most projects, as it adds elasticity to your edges, but if you're not comfortable using it, try working with a needle two sizes larger and working a regular longtail cast on.

Jeny's Surprisingly Stretchy Bind Off is a fabulous finishing technique, particularly for the lace projects in the book. Again, if you're not comfortable working JSS, work a regular bind off on needles a couple of sizes larger than your working needles.

- https://newstitchaday.com/twisted-german-cast-on-knitting
- http://knitty.com/ISSUEfall09/FEATjssbo.php

Unless specifically stated, always bind off in pattern—it gives a more cohesive, polished edging, and adds to the elasticity of your work.

GAUGE

I give gauge and needle recommendations throughout the book, however, I strongly encourage you to take gauge with a pinch of salt. Experiment! Go up a few needle sizes and see what kind of blocked fabric you create, or go down a needle size. Stretch the boundaries of conventional gauge and see what you produce. Be sure to block though, as what's on your needles can vastly differ to the finished blocked version.

CABLES

I'm a strong proponent of cabling without a cable needle, and list cable needles as optional throughout the book. If you haven't tried cabling without a needle, you'll find the scarves in this book to be the perfect projects to master this skill. Choose a yarn that has some wool in it, and consider working with wooden needles, which have a bit more "tooth" to grab onto your stitches. You'll be cabling without a needle in no time.

DIRECTIONS AND PHRASES USED IN THE BOOK

- Work sts as they appear—this is usually a direction for the WS of your work and means to knit the knit stitches and purl the purl stitches.
- Work as set—this direction is given once you've established your pattern placement on your stitches - for example, if you have four garter stitches,

27 pattern stitches, followed by a further 4 garter sts, then every row will follow this sequence.

- Follow chart or written version—every pattern here is presented both fully written out and also in a condensed version with charts. Both give the same directions for the same end result.
- Bind off in pattern—this means that whatever pattern you've been working, continue to work that pattern for each stitch, then bind it off. For example, if you've been working a k1, p1 rib, then to bind off, you'd knit a stitch, purl a stitch, then bind off the knit stitch. Similarly, bind off knitwise, means knit all the stitches you're binding off.
- Weaving in ends—I like to weave in ends after blocking, but as long as you weave ends in on the wrong side of your work, and for at least 10 sts, you'll not have to worry about your ends coming unraveled.
- Blocking—Steam or wet blocking are your best choices to set those stitches in place and allow your yarn to bloom. Be sure to check the before and after blocking measurements for the scarf you're knitting; sometimes, there's a big difference.

DEDICATION

*To my
#TeamAwesome!
I love you! Whep!*

DEAR PRUDENCE

For the Dear Prudence scarf, I chose a simple, yet striking stitch pattern, paired with a worsted weight yarn to make those wrapped stitches really pop. This scarf is suited to most yarn weights, and dye styles—variegated, kettle-dyed, gradients, the choices are endless.

REQUIRED SKILLS

Basic knitting skills
German Twisted cast on
3 st wrap

MEASUREMENTS

Before blocking: 5.25 inches / 13.25 cm wide x 64 inches / 162.5 cm long
After blocking: 5.5 inches / 14 cm wide x 68 inches / 172.75 cm long

MATERIALS

Malabrigo Worsted (100% Merino; 210 yds / 192m per 100g skein); Periwinkle: 2 skeins, or 420 yds of any worsted weight yarn
US#8 / 5 mm needles
Large-eyed, blunt sewing needle

GAUGE

Before blocking: 32 sts x 24 rows = 4 inches / 10 cm in stitch pattern

SPECIAL STITCHES

3 st wrap - [wyib, slip next 3 sts to RH needle, bring yarn to front of work, slip 3 sts back to LH needle] 3 times, k1, p1, k1.

PATTERN NOTES

When working your wrap st, practice to see how you like your wraps to sit; loosely, at gauge, or tightly wrapped. Each gives a different effect, and all are delightful. See page 8 for info on cast ons.

PATTERN WITHOUT CHART

Using German Twisted, or your favorite stretchy method, cast on 37 sts. Work 5 inches / 12.5 cm of p1, k1 rib.

Row 1: P1, *k1, p1; repeat from * to end of row.

Row 2 (and all even rows): K1, *p1, k1; repeat from * to end of row.

DESIGN NOTES

Dear Prudence is based on a 37-stitch pattern made up of k1, p1 rib and wrapped sts, worked in a worsted weight yarn.

Row 3: P1, *3 st wrap, [p1, k1] 6 times, p1; repeat from * to last 4 sts, 3 st wrap, p1.

Row 5: P1, k1, p1, 3 st wrap, [p1, k1] 4 times, p1, 3 st wrap, p1, 3 st wrap, [p1, k1] 4 times, p1, 3 st wrap, p1, k1, p1.

Row 7: P1, 3 st wrap, p1, 3 st wrap, [p1, k1] twice, p1, [3 st wrap, p1] twice, 3 st wrap, [p1, k1] twice, p1, [3 st wrap, p1] twice.

Row 9: P1, k1, p1, *3 st wrap, p1; repeat from * to last 3 sts, p1, k1, p1.

Row 11: [P1, k1] twice, p1, [3 st wrap, p1] three times, [k1, p1] twice, [3 st wrap, p1] three times, [k1, p1] twice.

Row 13: [P1, k1] three times, p1, [3 st wrap, p1] twice, [k1, p1] 4 times, [3 st wrap, p1] twice, [k1, p1] three times.

Row 15: [P1, k1] four times, p1, 3 st wrap, [p1, k1] six times, p1, 3 st wrap, [p1, k1] four times, p1.

Rows 17 - 26: Repeat Rows 1 and 2.

Repeat Rows 1 - 26 until the scarf is 5 inches / 12.5 cm shorter than desired length, ending after Row 16.

Work 5 inches / 12.5 cm of p1, k1 rib. Bind off in pattern.

PATTERN WITH CHART

Using German Twisted, or your favorite stretchy method, cast on 37 sts.

Work 5 inches / 12.5 cm of p1, k1 rib, then work repeats of Dear Prudence chart until it is 5 inches / 12.5 cm shorter than desired length, ending after Row 16. Work a further 5 inches / 12.5 cm of p1, k1 rib, then bind off in pattern.

FINISHING

Weave in any ends, and wet block.

☐ RS: Knit   WS: Purl

⊡ RS: Purl   WS: Knit

⇄ 3 st wrap

DEAR PRUDENCE CHART

HONG KONG GARDEN

This sideways scarf is the perfect vehicle to highlight three mini skeins, a long-repeat gradient, or a busy variegated, thus making the scarf a versatile addition to your wardrobe.

REQUIRED SKILLS

Basic knitting skills
German Twisted cast on
3 st wrap

MEASUREMENTS

Before blocking: 6 inches / 15.25 cm wide x 54 inches / 137 cm long
After blocking: 6.25 inches / 16 cm wide x 70 inches / 177.75 cm long

MATERIALS

Anzula Squishy(80% Superwash merino, 10% Cashmere, 10% Nylon; 169 yds / 154 m per 50g skein); color: C1: Daffodil, C2: Echo, C3: Frankie; 1 skein of each, or approx 520 yds / 475.5 m of fingering weight yarn
US#4 / 3.5 mm circular needle
Stitch markers
Large-eyed, blunt sewing needle

GAUGE

Before blocking: 40 sts x 32 rows = 4 inches / 10 cm in stitch pattern

DESIGN NOTES

Worked sideways, Hong Kong Garden differs from Dear Prudence by the addition of columns of rib sts between the previous stitch pattern. To make your scarf wider, increase your cast on number by multiples of 38 sts, with each repeat measuring around 4 inches / 10.25 cm wide before blocking.

SPECIAL STITCHES

3 st wrap - [wyib, slip next 3 sts to RH needle, bring yarn to front of work, slip 3 sts back to LH needle] 3 times, k1, p1, k1.

PATTERN NOTES

With C1, and using German Twisted, or your favorite stretchy method, cast on 495 sts.

Row 1: *P1, k1; repeat from * to end of row, placing markers after every 38 sts to help keep track of repeats.

Row 2: *K1, p1; repeat from * to end of row, slipping markers as you come to them.

Rows 3 and 5: *P1, k1; repeat from * to end of row.

Row 4 (and all even rows): *K1, p1; repeat from * to end of row.

Row 7: P1, *3 st wrap, [p1, k1] 6 times, p1; repeat from * to last 5 sts, 3 st wrap, p1, k1.

Row 9: P1, k1, p1, 3 st wrap, [p1, k1] 4 times, p1, 3 st wrap, p1, 3 st wrap, [p1, k1] 4 times, p1, 3 st wrap, [p1, k1] twice.

Row 11: P1, 3 st wrap, p1, 3 st wrap, [p1, k1] twice, p1, [3 st wrap, p1] twice, 3 st wrap, [p1, k1] twice, p1, [3 st wrap, p1] twice, k1, p1.

Row 13: P1, k1, p1, *3 st wrap, p1; repeat from * to last 6 sts, [p1, k1] three times.

Row 15: [P1, k1] twice, p1, [3 st wrap, p1] three times, [k1, p1] twice, [3 st wrap, p1] three times, [k1, p1] three times.

Row 17: [P1, k1] three times, p1, [3 st wrap, p1] twice, [k1, p1] 4 times, [3 st wrap, p1] twice, [k1, p1] four times.

With C2, repeat Rows 1 - 20.
With C3, repeat Rows 1 - 20.
Bind off in pattern.
See page 8 for info on cast on

PATTERN WITH CHART

With C1, and using German Twisted, or your favorite stretchy method, cast on 495 sts.
Work Row 1 of the Hong Kong Garden chart, placing a stitch marker after every 38 sts to help you mark your repeats.
Continue in this manner through Row 20 of your pattern, then repeat Rows 1 - 20 with C2, then Rows 1 - 20 with C3.
Bind off in pattern.

FINISHING

Weave in any ends, and wet block.

HONG KONG GARDEN CHART

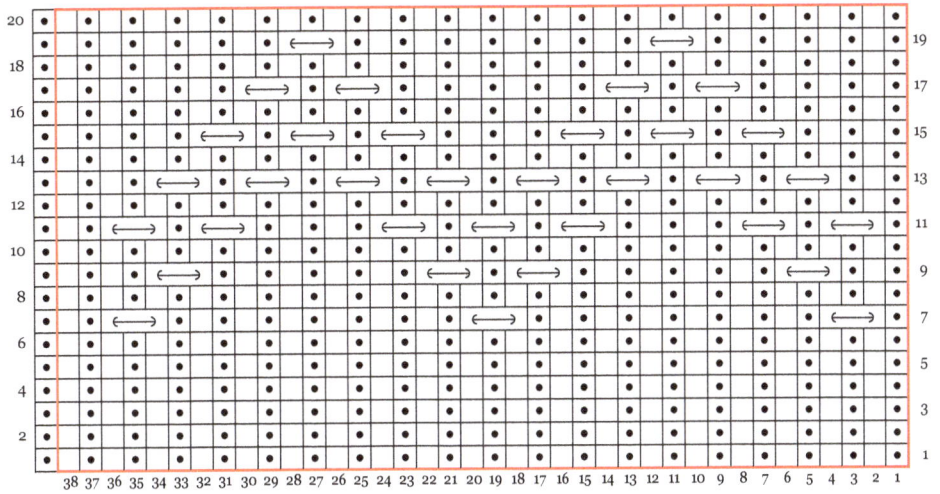

☐ RS: Knit   WS: Purl

▪ RS: Purl   WS: Knit

⟷ 3 st wrap

☐ Repeat

PEEK-A-BOO

A simple cable and wrap stitch combo create a chain effect that suits this heathered yarn perfectly.

REQUIRED SKILLS
Basic knitting skills
Simple cables
4 st wrap

MEASUREMENTS
Before blocking: 6 inches / 15.25 cm wide x 54 inches / 137 cm long
After blocking: 7 inches / 17.75 cm wide x 54 inches / 137 cm long

MATERIALS
Youghiogheny Highlands DK (85% Merino, 15% Nylon; 230 yds / 210 m per 100g skein); color: Not So Drab; 2 skeins, or 460 yds / 420.75 m of any DK weight yarn
US#8 / 5 mm needle
Cable needle (optional)
Large-eyed, blunt sewing needle

GAUGE
Before blocking: 18 sts x 24 rows = 4 inches / 10 cm in stitch pattern

SPECIAL STITCHES
4 st wrap - wyib, [slip next 4 sts to RH needle, bring yarn to front, slip 4 sts back to LH needle, wrapping yarn around sts as you bring it to the back] three times, k4.
2/1 LpC - slip next 2 sts to cn, hold in front of work, p1, k2 from cn
2/1 RpC - slip next st to cn, hold in back of work, k2, p1 from cn

DESIGN NOTES
The Peek-A-Boo scarf is based off an 11 st pattern, bordered by an 8 st column on either side. To make the scarf wider, add multiples of 11 to the cast on number.

PATTERN WITHOUT CHART
Using German Twisted, or your favorite stretchy method, cast on 50 sts.

Row 1: [P2, k2] twice, p1, [k2, p2, k2, p2, k2, p1] three times, [k2, p2] twice.

Row 2 (and all even rows): Work sts as they appear.

Repeat Rows 1 and 2 four more times, for a total of 10 rows worked.

Row 11: P2, 2/1 LpC, 2/1 RpC, [p1, 2/1 LpC, 2/1 RpC, p2, k2] three times, 2/1 LpC, 2/1 RpC, p2.

Row 13: P3, 4 st wrap, p1, [p2, 4 st wrap, p3, k2] three times, p2, 4 st wrap, p3.

Row 15: P2, 2/1 RpC, 2/1 LpC, p1, [2/1 RpC, 2/1 LpC, p2, k2, p1] three times, 2/1 RpC, 2/1 LpC, p2.

Row 17: P2, 2/1 LpC, 2/1 RpC, [p1, k2, p2, 2/1 LpC, 2/1 RpC] three times, 2/1 RpC, 2/1 LpC, p2.

Row 19: P3, 4 st wrap, [p2, k2, p3, 4 st wrap] three times, p3, 4 st wrap, p3.

Row 21: P2, 2/1 RpC, 2/1 LpC, p1, [k2, p2, 2/1 RpC, 2/1 LpC] three times, p1, 2/1 RpC, 2/1 LpC, p2.

Row 23: P2, 2/1 LpC, 2/1 RpC, p1, [2/1 LpC, 2/1 RpC, p2, k2] three times, p1, 2/1 LpC, 2/1 RpC, p2.

Row 25: P3, 4 st wrap, p2, [p1, 4 st wrap, p3, k2, p1] three times, p1, 4 st wrap, p3.

Row 27: P2, 2/1 RpC, 2/1 LpC, p1, [2/1 RpC, 2/1 LpC, p2, k2 p1] three times, 2/1 RpC, 2/1 LpC, p2.

Row 29: P2, 2/1 LpC, 2/1 RpC, p1, [k2, p2, 2/1 LpC, 2/1 RpC, p1] three times, 2/1 LpC, 2/1 RpC, p2.

Row 31: P3, 4 st wrap, p2, [k2, p3, 4 st wrap, p2] three times, 4 st wrap, p3.

Row 33: P2, 2/1 RpC, 2/1 LpC, p1, [k2, p2, 2/1 RpC, 2/1 LpC, p1] three times, 2/1 RpC, 2/1 LpC, p2.

Row 34: As Row 2.

Repeat Rows 11 - 34 until your scarf is about 2 inches / 5 cm shorter than desired length, then work Rows 1 and 2 five times. Bind off in pattern.

PATTERN WITH CHART

Using German Twisted, or your favorite stretchy method, cast on 50 sts.

Row 1: [P2, k2] twice, p1, [k2, p2, k2, p2, k2, p1] three times, [k2, p2] twice.
Row 2: Work sts as they appear.

Repeat Rows 1 and 2 four more times, for a total of 10 rows worked.

Work repeats of the pattern from Peek-A-Boo chart until it is 2 inches / 5 cm shorter than desired length, ending after Row 24.

Work Rows 1 and 2 four more times, then bind off in pattern.

FINISHING

Weave in any ends, and wet block.

☐ RS: Knit   WS: Purl

• RS: Purl   WS: Knit

2/1 LpC

2/1 RpC

4 st wrap

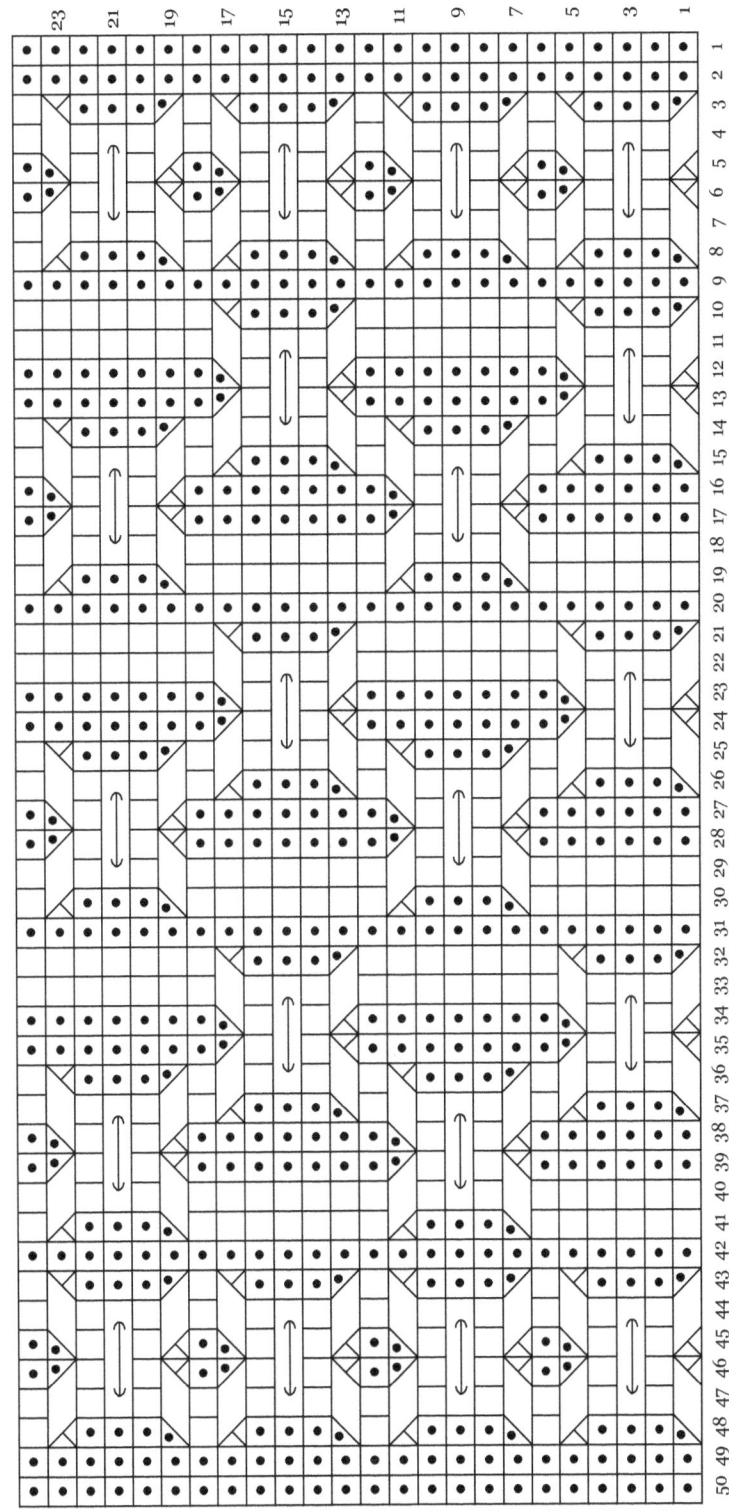

PEEK-A-BOO CHART

DIZZY

Deliberately worked looser than an average gauge for sport weight yarn, the drape of Dizzy works perfectly with this stitch pattern to create a neck wrap that's just the right touch of luxury...

REQUIRED SKILLS

Basic knitting skills
Simple cables
4 st wrap

MEASUREMENTS

Before blocking: 23 inches / 58.5 cm wide x 5.5 inches / 14 cm high
After blocking: 28 inches / 71 cm wide x 6 inches / 15.25 cm high

MATERIALS

Dragonfly Fibers Damsel Sport (100% Merino; 335 yds / 306 m per 115 g / 4.06 oz skein); Cheshire Cat: 1 skeins - or about 200 yds / xx m of any sport weight yarn
US#7/ 4.5 mm needle
Cable needle (optional)
Large-eyed, blunt sewing needle

GAUGE

Before blocking: 28 sts x 24 rows = 4 inches / 10 cm in stitch pattern

DESIGN NOTES

Again, knitted sideways, this 11 st pattern repeat is bordered by 8 st columns either side to provide a little structure. To make Dizzy wider, or narrower, increase or decrease the cast on number by multiples of 11 sts.

SPECIAL STITCHES

4 st wrap - wyib, [slip next 4 sts to RH needle, bring yarn to front, slip 4 sts back to LH needle, wrapping yarn around sts as you bring it to the back] three times, k4.
2/1 LpC - slip next 2 sts to cn, hold in front of work, p1, k2 from cn
2/1 RpC - slip next st to cn, hold in back of work, k2, p1 from cn

PATTERN WITHOUT CHART

Using long tail method, cast on 193 sts.

Row 1: [P2, k2] twice, p1, [k2, p2, k2, p2, k2, p1] sixteen times, [k2, p2] twice.

Row 2 (and all even rows): Work sts as they appear.

Row 3: P2, 2/1 LpC, 2/1 RpC, p1, k2, p1, [2/1 LpC, 2/1 RpC, p2, k2, p1] sixteen times, 2/1 LpC, 2/1 RpC, p2.

Row 5: P3, 4 st wrap, p1, [p2, 4 st wrap, p3, k2] sixteen times, p2, 4 st wrap, p3.

Row 7: P2, 2/1 RpC, 2/1 LpC, p1, [2/1 RpC, 2/1 LpC, p2, k2, p1] sixteen times, 2/1 RpC, 2/1 LpC, p2.

Row 9: P2, 2/1 LpC, 2/1 RpC, p1, [k2, p2, 2/1 LpC, 2/1 RpC, p1] sixteen times, 2/1 LpC, 2/1 RpC, p2.

Row 11: P3, 4 st wrap, p1, [p1, k2, p3, 4 st wrap, p1] sixteen times, p2, 4 st wrap, p3.

Row 13: P2, 2/1 RpC, 2/1 LpC, p1, [k2, p2, 2/1 RpC, 2/1 LpC] sixteen times, p1, 2/1 RpC, 2/1 LpC, p2.

Row 15: P2, 2/1 LpC, 2/1 RpC, p1, [2/1 LpC, 2/1 RpC, p2, k2] sixteen times, p1, 2/1 LpC, 2/1 RpC, p2.

Row 17: P3, 4 st wrap, p2, [p1, 4 st wrap, p3, k2, p1] sixteen times, p1, 4 st wrap, p3.

Row 19: P2, 2/1 RpC, 2/1 LpC, p1, [2/1 RpC, 2/1 LpC, p2, k2 p1] sixteen times, 2/1 RpC, 2/1 LpC, p2.

Row 21: P2, 2/1 LpC, 2/1 RpC, p1, [k2, p2, 2/1 LpC, 2/1 RpC, p1] sixteen times, 2/1 LpC, 2/1 RpC, p2.

Row 23: P3, 4 ssh wrap, p2, [k2, p3, 4 st wrap, p2] sixteen times, 4 st wrap, p3.

Row 25: P2, 2/1 RpC, 2/1 LpC, p1, [k2, p2, 2/1 RpC, 2/1 LpC, p1] sixteen times, 2/1 RpC, 2/1 LpC, p2.

Row 26: As Row 2.

Repeat Rows 2 - 26 four times. Work Rows 1 and 2.
Bind off in pattern.

PATTERN WITH CHART

Using long tail method, cast on 193 sts.
Work Rows 1 - 26 of Dizzy chart once, repeating the sts within the red box a total of 16 times on each row, then repeats of Rows 3 - 26 three times. Work Rows 1 and 2 once. Bind off.

FINISHING

Weave in any ends, and wet block.

DIZZY CHART

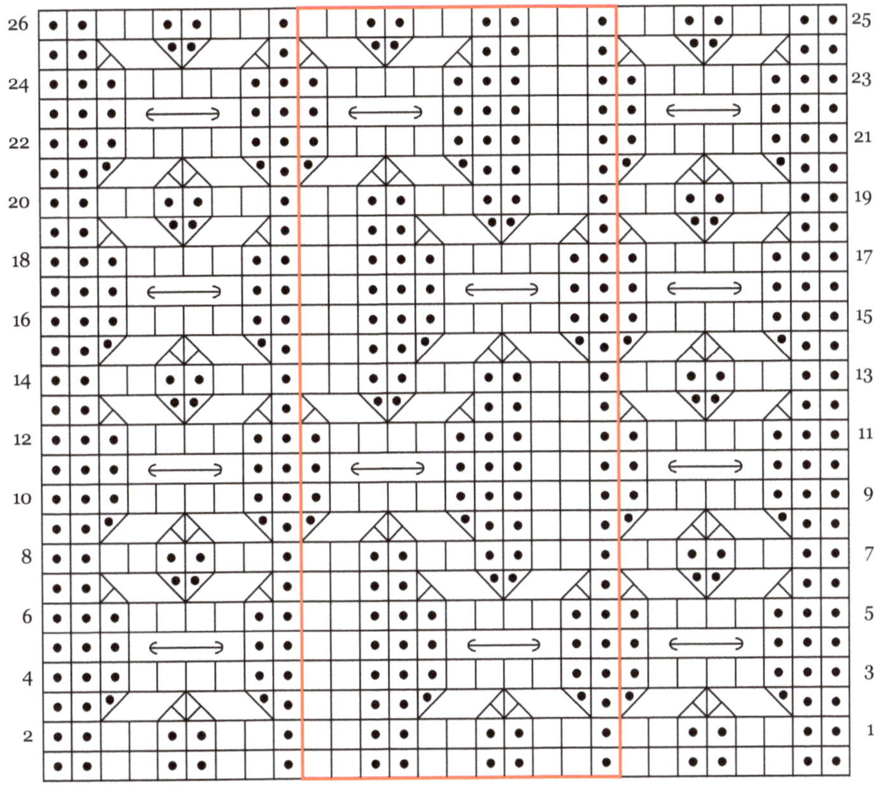

25

- ☐ RS: Knit WS: Purl
- ▪ RS: Purl WS: Knit
- 2/1 LpC
- 2/1 RpC
-  4 st wrap
- Repeat

HAPPY HOUSE

This easy-to-memorize pattern is beautifully leafy and springlike.

REQUIRED SKILLS

Basic knitting skills
Simple lace

MEASUREMENTS

Before blocking: 7 inches / 17.75 cm wide x 66 inches / 167.75 cm high
After blocking: 7.5 inches / 19 cm wide x 68 inches / 172.75 cm high

MATERIALS

Spunky Eclectic Super DK (100% Merino; 280 yds / 256m per 100g skein); color: Ginkgo; 2 skeins, or about 420 yds / 384 m of DK weight yarn
US#8 / 5 mm needle
Large-eyed, blunt sewing needle

GAUGE

Before blocking: 24 sts x 28 rows = 4 inches / 10 cm in stitch pattern

SPECIAL STITCHES

CDD - slip 1, k2tog, psso

PATTERN WITHOUT CHART

Using long tail method, cast on 37 sts.

Rows 1 - 6: Knit.

Row 7: K3, [p1, ssk, k2, yo, k1, yo, k2, k2tog] three times, p1, k3.

Row 8 (and all even rows): K4, [p9, k1] three times, k3.

Row 9: As Row 7.

Row 11: As Row 7.

Row 13: K3, [p1, yo, ssk, k5, k2tog, yo] three times, p1, k3.

Row 15: K3, [p1, k1, yo, ssk, k3, k2tog, yo, k1] three times, p1, k3.

Row 17: K3, [p1, k2, yo, ssk, k1, k2tog, yo, k2] three times, p1, k3.

Row 19: K3, [p1, k3, yo, cdd, yo, k3]

DESIGN NOTES

I added a garter stitch border all around this lace pattern, both to pleasingly frame it, and also to eliminate the curl that happens with a stockinette based stitch pattern.

three times, p1, k3.

Row 20: As Row 8.

Repeat Rows 7 - 20 until desired length is reached, or you almost run out of yarn. Work Rows 1 - 6 once, then bind off knitwise.

PATTERN WITH CHART

Using long tail method, cast on 37 sts. Rows 1 - 6: Knit.

Work Rows 1 - 20 of Happy House chart, repeating the sts within the red box three times. When scarf is almost as long as you'd like, work Rows 1 - 6 once more. Bind off knitwise.

HAPPY HOUSE CHART

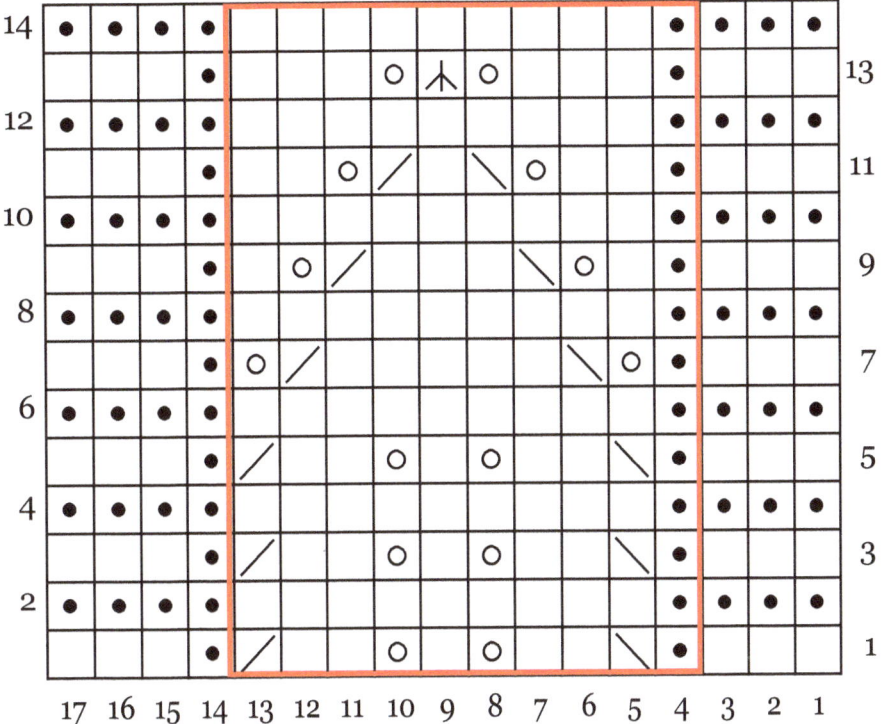

☐ RS: Knit WS: Purl

• RS: Purl WS: Knit

○ Yarn over

╱ K2tog

╲ Ssk

⋏ Sl1, k2tog, psso

☐ Repeat

ARABIAN NIGHTS

Silk adds drape and weight to this scarf as well as softness and warmth. You'll love the easy to memorize repeats.

DESIGN NOTES

Worked at a very loose gauge, to enhance the drapey lace, the stitch patt was repeated 5 times. To make a wider or narrower scarf, decrease or add multiples of 10 sts.

REQUIRED SKILLS

Basic knitting skills
Simple lace

MEASUREMENTS

Before blocking: 10 inches / 25.5 cm wide x 54 inches / 137.25 cm high
After blocking: 11.5 inches / 29.25 cm wide x 67 inches / 170.25 cm high

MATERIALS

Alchemy Yarns of Transformation Lust (70% wool, 30% silk; 253 yds / 231m per 53g skein); Pyrite: 2 skeins, or approx. 500 yds / 457 m of fingering weight yarn
US#8 / 5 mm needle
Large-eyed, blunt sewing needle

GAUGE

Before blocking: 24 sts x 28 rows = 4 inches / 10 cm in stitch pattern

SPECIAL STITCHES

CDD - slip 1, k2tog, psso

PATTERN WITHOUT CHART

Using long tail method, cast on 57 sts.

Row 1: K3, [p1, ssk, k2, yo, k1, yo, k2, k2tog] five times, p1, k3.

Row 2 (and all even rows): K4, [p9, k1] five times, k3.

Row 3: As Row 7.

Row 5: As Row 7.

Row 7: K3, [p1, yo, ssk, k5, k2tog, yo] five times, p1, k3.

Row 9: K3, [p1, k1, yo, ssk, k3, k2tog, yo, k1] five times, p1, k3.

Row 11: K3, [p1, k2, yo, ssk, k1, k2tog, yo, k2] five times, p1, k3.

Row 13: K3, [p1, k3, yo, cdd, yo, k3] five times, p1, k3.

Row 14: As Row 8.

Repeat Rows 1 - 14 until desired length is reached, or you almost run out of yarn. Bind off in pattern.

PATTERN WITH CHART

Using long tail method, cast on 57 sts.

Work Rows 1 - 14 of Arabian Nights chart, repeating the sts in the red box five times. Bind off in pattern.

FINISHING

Weave in any ends, and wet block.

ARABIAN NIGHTS CHART

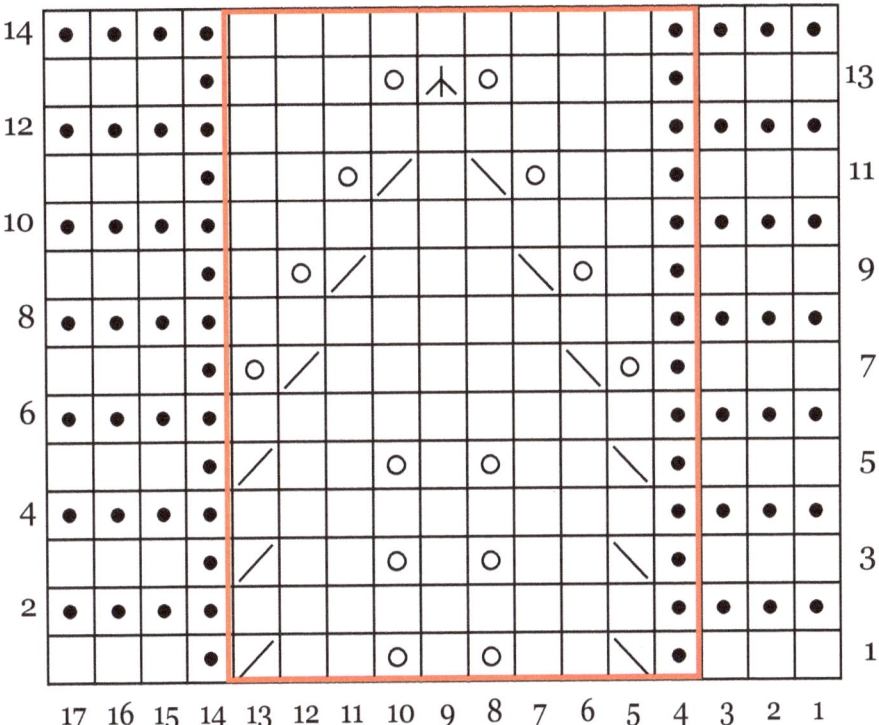

☐ RS: Knit WS: Purl

● RS: Purl WS: Knit

○ Yarn over

╱ K2tog

╲ Ssk

⋏ Sl1, k2tog, psso

☐ Repeat

KISS THEM FOR ME

Ross Farm is one of the foremost promoters of Leicester Longwool sheep in the United States. Excellent stitch definition and drape in this scarf!

REQUIRED SKILLS

Intermediate knitting skills
Increases / decreases
3 st wrap
Bobble

MEASUREMENTS

Before blocking: 5 inches / x 12.75 cm wide x 71.5 inches / 181.5 cm high
After blocking: 6 inches / 15.25 cm wide x 74 inches / 188 cm high

MATERIALS

Ross Farms Leicester Longwool Sport (100% Leicester Longwool; approx. 250 yds / 228 m per 135g skein); color: Natural; 2 skeins, or 500 yds / 458 m of any sport weight yarn
US#6 / 4 mm needle
Large-eyed, blunt sewing needle

GAUGE

Before blocking: 30 sts x 32 rows = 4 inches / 10 cm in stitch pattern

DESIGN NOTES

This scarf is created using one repeat of a 24 st cable and lace pattern, edged either side by an 8 st bobbled column.

SPECIAL STITCHES

3 st wrap - [wyib, slip next 3 sts to RH needle, bring yarn to front of work, slip 3 sts back to LH needle] 3 times, k1, p1, k1.
B - bobble - (k, p, k, p, k) into next st, turn, p5, turn, k2tog, k3tog, pass k2tog over k3tog

PATTERN NOTES

Don't worry if your bobbles appear to sink into the back of your work as you knit them. This is easily fixed in blocking. Simply pop them to the front during blocking, and they'll set in place.

There are many different ways to create a bobble, choose your favorite one, or avoid the bobbles altogether and go with a bead, or just a knit stitch instead.

Throughout the pattern, on WS rows, you'll have two yarn over increases. Yarnovers between two knit stitches should be ktbl, yarnovers between a knit and purl stitch should be ptbl.

On Rows 13 and 33, you'll be working a yarn over right before a 3 st wrap. It's slightly tricky to work, just be sure to allow slightly more ease on your yarn over than you typically would, since it's going to stretch over 3 sts.

PATTERN WITHOUT CHART

Using German Twisted, or your favorite stretchy method, cast on 41 sts.

Row 1: P1, k1tbl, kpk1, k2, B, k2, p6, k2tog, [p1, k1tbl] twice, yo, p1, yo, [k1tbl, p1] twice, ssk, p6, k2, B, k2, p1, k1tbl, p1.

Row 2 (and all even rows): Work sts as they appear. (see above for notes about working yarn overs).

Row 3: p1, k1tbl, p1, yo, ssk, p1, k2tog, yo, p5, k2tog, [p1, k1tbl] twice, yo, k1tbl, p1, k1tbl, yo, [k1tbl, p1] twice, ssk, p5, yo, ssk, p1, k2tog, yo, p1, k1tbl, p1l.

Row 5: P1, k1tbl, [p1, k2] twice, p4, k2tog, [p1, k1tbl] twice, yo, p1, 3 st wrap, p1, yo, [k1tbl, p1] twice, ssk, p4, [k2, p1] twice, k1tbl, p1.

Row 7: P1, k1tbl, p1, k2tog, yo, p1, yo, ssk, p3, k2tog, [p1, k1tbl] twice, yo, [k1tbl, p1] three times, k1tbl, yo, [k1tbl, p1] twice, ssk, p3, k2tog, yo, p1, yo, ssk, p1, k1tbl, p1.

Row 9: P1, k1tbl, p1, k2, B, k2, p2, k2tog, [p1, k1tbl] twice, yo, [p1, 3 st wrap] twice, p1, yo,]k1tbl, p1] twice, ssk, p2, k2, B, k2, p1, k1tbl, p1.

Row 11: P1, k1tbl, p1, yo, ssk, p1, k2tog, yo, p1, k2tog, [p1, k1tbl] twice, yo, [k1tbl, p1] five times, k1tbl, yo, [k1tbl, p1] twice, ssk, p1, yo, ssk, p1, k2tog, yo, p1, k1tbl, p1.

Row 13: P1, k1tbl, p1, [k2, p1] twice, ssk, [k1tbl, p1] twice, yo, [3 st wrap, p1] twice, 3 st wrap, yo, [p1, k1tbl] twice, k2tog, [p1, k2] twice, p1, k1tbl, p1.

Row 15: P1, k1tbl, p1, k2tog, yo, p1, yo, [ssk, p1] twice, k1tbl, p1, k1tbl, yo, [k1tbl, p1] five times, k1tbl, yo, [k1tbl, p1] twice, k2tog, p1, k2tog, yo, p1, yo, ssk, p1, k1tbl, p1.

Row 17: P1, k1tbl, p1, k2, B, k2, p1, ssk, [k1tbl, p1] twice, yo, k1tbl, p1, [3 st wrap, p1] twice, k1tbl, yo, [p1, k1tbl] twice, k2tog, p1, k2, B, k2, p1, k1tbl, p1.

Row 19: P1, k1tbl, p1, yo, ssk, p1, k2tog, yo, p1, ssk, [p1, k1tbl] twice, yo, [k1tbl, p1] five times, k1tbl, yo, [k1tbl, p1] twice, k2tog, p1, yo, ssk, p1, k2tog, yo, p1, k1tbl, p1.

Row 21: P1, k1tbl, p1, k2, p1, k2, p6, k2tog, [p1, k1tbl] twice, yo, p1, yo, [k1tbl, p1] twice, ssk, p6, k2, p1, k2, p1, k1tbl, p1.

Row 23: P1, k1tbl, p1, k2tog, yo, p1, yo, ss, p5, k2tog, [p1, k1tbl] twice, yo, [k1tbl, p1] three times, k1tbl, yo, [k1tbl, p1] twice, ssk, p5, k2tog, yo, kpk1, yo, ssk, p1, k1tbl, p1.

Row 25: P1, k1tbl, p1, k2, B, k2, p4, k2tog, [p1, k1tbl] twice, yo, p1, 3 st wrap, p1, yo, [k1tbl, p1] twice, ssk, p4, k2, B, k2, p1, k1tbl, p1.

Row 27: P1, k1tbl, p1, yo, ssk, p1, k2tog, yo, p3, k2tog, [p1, k1tbl] twice, yo [k1tbl, p1] three times, k1tbl, yo, [k1tbl, p1] twice, ssk, p3, yo, ssk, p1, k2tog, yo, p1, k1tbl, p1.

Row 29: P1, k1tbl, p1, k2, p1, k2, p2, k2tog, [p1, k1tbl] twice, yo, [p1, 3 st wrap] twice, p1, yo, [k1tbl, p1] twice, ssk, p2, k2, p1, k2, p1, k1tbl, p1.

Row 31: P1, k1tbl, p1, k2tog, yo, p1, yo, ssk, p1, k2tog, [p1, k1tbl] twice, yo, [k1tbl, p1] five times, k1tbl, yo, [k1tbl, p1] twice, ssk, p1, k2tog, yo, p1, yo, ssk, p1, k1tbl, p1.

Row 33: P1, k1tbl, p1, k2, B, k2, p1, ssk, [k1tbl, p1] twice, yo, [3 st wrap, p1] twice, 3 st wrap, yo, [p1, k1tbl] twice, k2tog, p1, k2, B, k2, p1, k1tbl, p1.

Row 35: P1, k1tbl, p1, yo, ssk, p1, k2tog, yo, p1, ssk, [p1, k1tbl] twice, yo, [k1tbl, p1] five times, k1tbl, yo, [k1tbl, p1] twice, k2tog, p1, yo, ssk, p1, k2tog, yo, p1, k1tbl, p1.

Row 37: P1, k1tbl, p1, k2, p1, k2, p1, ssk, [k1tbl, p1] twice, yo, k1tbl, p1, [3 st wrap, p1] twice, k1tbl, yo, [p1, k1tbl] twice, k2tog, p1, k2, p1, k2, p1, k1tbl, p1.

Row 39: P1, k1tbl, p1, k2tog, yo, p1, yo, ssk, p1, ssk, [p1, k1tbl] twice, yo, [k1tbl, p1] five times, k1tbl, yo, [k1tbl, p1] twice, k2tog, p1, k2tog, yo, p1, yo, ssk, p1, k1tbl, p1.

Repeat Rows 1 - 40 until desired length is reached, ending after Row 20 or Row 40. Bind off in pattern.

PATTERN WITH CHART

Using German Twisted, or your favorite stretchy method, cast on 41 sts.

Work repeats of Kiss Them For Me charts A, B, and C until desired length is reached, ending after Row 20 or Row 40 of Chart B. Bind off in pattern.

FINISHING

Weave in any ends, and wet block.

□	RS: Knit WS: Purl
▢	RS: Purl WS: Knit
℟	RS: Ktbl WS: Ptbl
○	Yarn over
╱	K2tog
╲	Ssk
←→	3 st wrap
B	Bobble
□	Repeat

39

CHRISTINE

This color, Victorian Village, is one of my all-time favorite pinks and it inspired me to create a high-necked blouse shape in this smaller yet challenging scarflet.

REQUIRED SKILLS

Intermediate knitting skills
Increases / decreases
3 st wrap
Bobble

MEASUREMENTS

Before blocking: 20 inches / 50.75 cm wide x 8 inches / 20.25 cm high

MATERIALS

Neighborhood Fiber Co. Studio Chunky (100% Superwash Merino; 125 yds / 114 m per 113 g skein); color: Victorian Village; 2 skeins, or approx. 225 yds / 205 m of chunky wool
US#11 / 8 mm needle
Large-eyed, blunt sewing needle

GAUGE

Before blocking: 28 sts x 24 rows = 4 inches / 10 cm in stitch pattern
After blocking: 26 sts x 24 rows = 4 inches / 10 cm in stitch pattern

DESIGN NOTES

The original concept for this was to work 3 reps of the Kiss Them For Me stitch pattern, however, the measurements were not correct, so I added vertical columns of k1tbl, p1, which added to the overall aesthetic. To make a wider version of Christine, you need multiples of the 30 sts pattern, plus 8 plus 15.

SPECIAL STITCHES

3 st wrap - [wyib, slip next 3 sts to RH needle, bring yarn to front of work, slip 3 sts back to LH needle] 3 times, k1, p1, k1.

MCOB - make cast on bobble. Cast on next st as usual, turn, (k, yo, k, yo, k) into st, turn, p5, turn, k2tog, k3tog, pass k2tog over k2tog

B - bobble - (k, p, k, p, k) into next st, turn, p5, turn, k2tog, k3tog, pass k2tog over k3tog

PATTERN NOTES

The bobble cast on requires extra yarn. Consider working from two different skeins, or from both ends of working skein.

Don't worry if your bobbles appear to sink into the back of your work as you knit them. This is easily fixed in blocking. Simply pop them to the front during blocking, and they'll set in place.

There are many different ways to create a bobble, choose your favorite one, or avoid the bobbles altogether and go with a bead or a knit stitch instead.

Throughout the pattern, on WS rows, you'll have two yarn over increases. Yarnovers between two knit stitches should be ktbl, yarnovers between a knit and purl stitch should be ptbl.

On Rows 13 and 33, you'll be working a yarn over right before a 3 st wrap. It's slightly tricky to work, just be sure to allow slightly more ease on your yarn over than you typically would, since it's going to stretch over 3 sts.

PATTERN WITHOUT CHART

Using German Twisted, or your favorite stretchy method, *cast on 5 sts, MCOB; repeat from * eighteen times, then cast on a further 5 sts. 113 sts total.

Row 1(RS): P1, k1tbl, p1, k5, *[p1, k1tbl] three times, p6, k2tog, [p1, k1tbl] twice, yo p1, yo, [k1tbl, p1] twice, ssk, p5; repeat from * to last 15 sts, [p1, k1tbl] three times, p1, k5, p1, k1tbl, p1.

Row 2 (and all even rows): Work sts as they appear. (see above for notes about working yarn overs).

Row 3: P1, k1tbl, p1, yo, ssk, p1, k2tog, yo, *[p1, k1tbl] three times, p5, k2tog, [p1, k1tbl] twice, k1tbl, yo, k1tbl, p1, k1tbl, yo, [k1tbl, p1] twice, ssk, p4; repeat from * to last 15 sts, [p1, k1tbl] three times, p1, yo, ssk, p1, k2tog, yo, p1, k1tbl, p1.

Row 5: P1, k1tbl, p1, k2, p1, k2, *[p1, k1tbl] three times, p4, k2tog, [p1, k1tbl] twice, yo, p1, 3 st wrap, p1, yo, [k1tbl, p1] twice, ssk, p3; repeat from * to last 15 sts, [p1, k1tbl] three times, p1, k2, p1, k2, p1, k1tbl, p1.

Row 7: P1, k1tbl, p1, k2tog, yo, p1, yo, ssk, *[p1, k1tbl] three times, p3, k2tog, [p1, k1tbl] twice, yo, [k1tbl, p1] three times, k1tbl, yo, [k1tbl, p1] twice, ssk, p2; repeat from * to last 15 sts, [p1, k1tbl] three times, p1, k2tog, yo, p1, yo, ssk, p1, 1tbl, p1.

Row 9: P1, k1tbl, p1, k2, MB, k2, *[p1, k1tbl] three times, p2, k2tog, [p1, k1tbl] twice, yo, [p1, 3 st wrap] twice, p1, yo, [k1tbl, p1] twice, ssk, p1; repeat from * to last 15 sts, [p1, k1tbl] three times, p1, k2, MB, k2, p1, k1tbl, p1.

Row 11: P1, k1tbl, p1, yo, ssk, p1, k2tog, yo, *[p1, k1tbl] three times, p1, k2tog, [p1, k1tbl] twice, yo, [k1tbl, p1] five times, k1tbl, yo, [k1tbl, p1] twice, ssk; repeat from * to last 15 sts, [p1, k1tbl] three times, p1, yo, ssk, p1, k2tog, yo, p1, k1tbl, p1.

Row 13: P1, k1tbl, [p1, k2] twice, *[p1, k1tbl] three times, p1, ssk, [k1tbl, p1] twice, yo, [3 st wrap, p1] twice, 3 st wrap, yo, [p1, k1tbl] twice, k2tog; repeat from * to last 15 sts, [p1, k1tbl] three times, [p1, k2] twice, p1, k1tbl, p1.

Row 15: P1, k1tbl, p1, k2tog, yo, p1, yo, ssk, *[p1, k1tbl] three times, p1, ssk, [p1, k1tbl] twice, yo, [k1tbl, p1] five times, k1tbl, yo, [k1tbl, p1] twice, k2tog; repeat from * to last 15 sts, [p1, k1tbl] three times, p1, k2tog, yo, p1, yo, ssk, p1, k1tbl, p1.

Row 17: P1, k1tbl, p1, k2, MB, k2; *[p1, k1tbl] three times, p1, ssk, [k1tbl, p1] twice, yo, k1tbl, [p1, 3 st wrap] twice, p1, k1tbl, yo, [p1, k1tbl] twice, k2tog; repeat from * to last 15 sts, [p1, k1tbl] three times, p1, k2, MB, k2, p1, k1tbl, p1.

Row 19: P1, k1tbl, p1, yo, ssk, p1, k2tog, yo, *[p1, k1tbl] three times, p1, ssk, [p1, k1tbl] twice, yo, [k1tbl, p1] five times, k1tbl, yo, [k1tbl, p1] twice, k2tog; repeat from * to last 15 sts, [p1, k1tbl] three times, p1, yo, ssk, p1, k2tog, yo, p1, k1tbl, p1.

Row 21: P1, k1tbl, [p1, k2] twice, *[p1, k1tbl] three times, p6, k2tog, [p1, k1tbl] twice, yo, p1, yo, [k1tbl, p1] twice, ssk, p5; repeat from * to last 15 sts, [p1, k1tbl] three times, [p1, k2] twice, p1, k1tbl, p1.

Row 23: P1, k1tbl, p1, k2tog, yo, p1, yo, ssk, *[p1, k1tbl] three times, p5, k2tog, [p1, k1tbl] twin, yo, k1tbl, p1, k1tbl, yo, [k1tbl, p1] twice, ssk, p4; repeat from * to last 15 sts, [p1, k1tbl] three times, p1, k2tog, yo, p1, yo, ssk, p1, k1tbl, p1.

Row 25: P1, k1tbl, p1, k2, MB, k2, *[p1, k1tbl] three times, p4, k2tog, [p1, k1tbl] twice, yo, p1, 3 st wrap, p1, yo, [k1tbl, p1] twice, ssk, p3; repeat from * to last 15 sts, [p1, k1tbl] three times, p1, k2, MB, k2, p1, k1tbl, p1.

Row 27: P1, k1tbl, p1, yo, ssk, p1, k2tog, yo, *[p1, k1tbl] three times, p3, k2tog, [p1, k1tbl] twice, yo, [k1tbl, p1] three times, k1tbl, yo, [k1tbl, p1] twice, ssk, p2; repeat from * to last 15 sts, [p1, k1tbl] three times, p1, yo, ssk, p1, k2tog, yo, p1, k1tbl, p1.

Row 29: P1, k1tbl, [p1, k2] twice, *[p1, k1tbl] three times, p2, k2tog, [p1, k1tbl] twice, yo, [p1, 3 st wrap] twice, p1, yo, [k1tbl, p1] twice, ssk, p1; repeat from * to last 15 sts, [p1, k1tbl] three times, [p1, k2] twice, p1, k1tbl, p1.

Row 31: P1, k1tbl, p1, k2tog, yo, p1, yo, ssk, *[p1, k1tbl] three times, p1, k2tog, [p1, k1tbl] twice, yo, [k1tbl, p1] five times, k1tbl, yo, [k1tbl, p1] twice, ssk; repeat from * to last 15 sts, [p1, k1tbl] three times, p1, k2tog, yo, p1, yo, ssk, p1, k1tbl, p1.

Row 33: P1, k1tbl, p1, k2, MB, k2, *[p1, k1tbl] three times, p1, ssk, [k1tbl, p1] twice, yo, [3 st wrap, p1] twice, 3 st wrap, yo, [p1, k1tbl] twice, k2tog; repeat from * to last 15 sts, [p1, k1tbl] three times, p1, k2, MB, k2, p1, k1tbl, p1.

Row 35: P1, k1tbl, p1, yo, ssk, p1, k2tog, yo, *[p1, k1tbl] three times, p1, ssk, [p1, k1tbl] twice, yo, [k1tbl, p1] five times, k1tbl, yo, [k1tbl, p1] twice, k2tog; repeat from * to last 15 sts, [p1, k1tbl] three times, p1, yo, ssk, p1, k2tog, yo, p1, k1tbl, p1.

Row 37: P1, k1tbl, [p1, k2] twice, *[p1, k1tbl] three times, p1, ssk, [k1tbl, p1] twice, yo, k1tbl, [p1, 3 st wrap] twice, p1, k1tbl, yo, [p1, k1tbl] twice, k2tog; repeat from * to last 15 sts, [p1, k1tbl] three times, [p1, k2] twice, p1, k1tbl, p1.

Row 39: P1, k1tbl, p1, k2tog, yo, p1, yo, ssk, *[p1, k1tbl] three times, p1, ssk, [p1, k1tbl] twice, yo, [k1tbl, p1] five times, k1tbl, yo, [k1tbl, p1] twice, k2tog; repeat from * to last 15 sts, [p1, k1tbl] three times, p1, k2tog, yo, p1, yo, ssk, p1, k1tbl, p1.

Row 40: As Row 2.

Bind off in pattern, and working a bobble every 6th st, before binding off that stitch.

PATTERN WITH CHART

Using German Twisted, or your favorite stretchy method, *cast on 5 sts, MCOB; repeat from * eighteen times, then cast on a further 5 sts. 113 sts total.

Work Row 1 of Christine charts in the following order: Chart A, Chart B three times, Chart C. Continue as established, working repeats of the red boxes within Charts A and C, and full repeats of Chart B until 40 rows have been completed.

Bind off, working a MB stitch every 6th stitch before binding it off.

FINISHING

Weave in any ends, and wet block. Close using a shawl pin or consider creating a crocheted loop to anchor to a button.

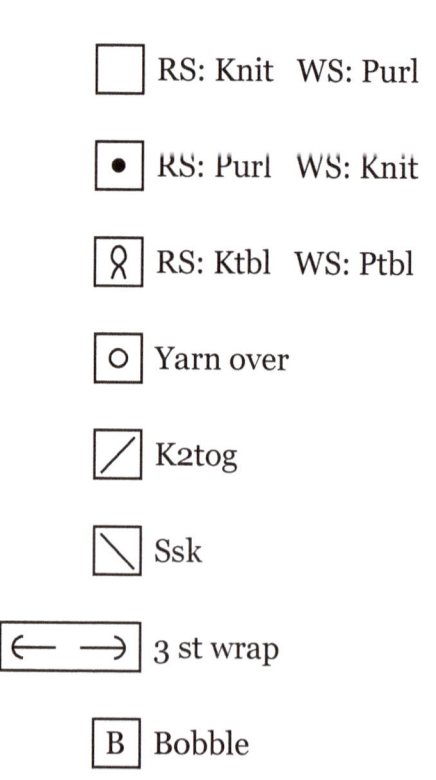

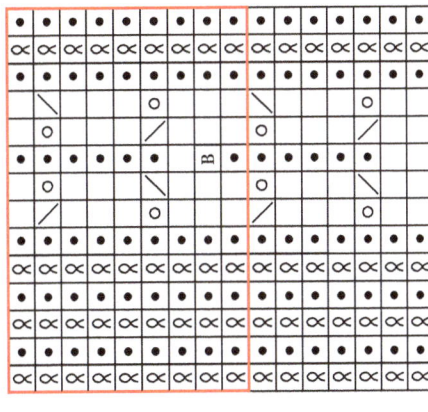

SLOWDIVE

Multicolored yarns often get lost in lace work or muddle the pattern visually but Malabrigo Rios yarn offers some great colorways such as this one where it actually highlights the lace rather than competing with it.

REQUIRED SKILLS

Intermediate knitting skills
Increases / decreases

MEASUREMENTS

Before blocking: 7 inches / 17.75 cm wide x 57 inches / 144.75 cm high
After blocking: 7 inches / 17.75 cm wide x 64 inches / 162.25 cm high

MATERIALS

Malabrigo Yarns Rios (100% Merino; 210 yds / 192 m per 100 skein); color: #859 Primavera; 2 skeins, or approx. 420 yds / 384 m of worsted weight yarn
US#8 / 5 mm needle
Large-eyed, blunt sewing needle

GAUGE

Before blocking: 24 sts x 28 rows = 4 inches / 10 cm in stitch pattern

DESIGN NOTES

A 27 st pattern, bordered by a 4 st garter edging to eliminate curl and frame the lace.

PATTERN WITHOUT CHART

Using long tail method, cast on 35 sts.

Rows 1 - 6: Knit.

Row 7: K3, p1, yo, ssk, yo, k1, CDD, k1, yo, k2tog, yo, k2, yo, k2tog, p1, ssk, yo, k2, yo, ssk, yo, k1, CDD, k1, yo, k2tog, yo, p1, k3.

Row 8 (and all even rows): K4, p13, k1, p13, k4.

Row 9: K3, p1, k1, yo, ssk, yo, CDD, yo, k2tog, yo, k3, yo, k2tog, p1, ssk, yo, k3, yo, ssk, yo, CDD, yo, k2tog, yo, k1, p1, k3.

Row 11: K3, p1, k2, yo, ssk, k1, k2tog, yo, k4, yo, k2tog, p1, ssk, yo, k4, yo, ssk, k1, k2tog, yo, k2, p1, k3.

Row 13: K3, p1, yo, ssk, k1, yo, CDD, yo, k5, yo, k2tog, p1, ssk, yo, k5, yo, k3tog, yo, k1, k2tog, yo, p1, k3.

Row 15: K3, p1, yo, ssk, k2, yo, ssk, yo, k1, CDD, k1, yo, k2tog, yo, p1, yo, ssk, yo, k1, CDD, k1, yo, k2tog, yo, k2, k2tog, yo, p1, k3.

Row 17: K3, p1, yo, ssk, k3, yo, ssk, yo, CDD, yo, k2tog, yo, k1, p1, k1, yo, ssk, yo, CDD, yo, k2tog, yo, k3, k2tog, yo, p1, k3.

Row 19: K3, p1, yo, ssk, k4, yo, ssk, k1, k2tog, yo, k2, p1, k2, yo, ssk, k1, k2tog, yo, k4, k2tog, yo, p1, k3.

Row 21: K3, p1, yo, ss, k5, yo, k3tog, yo, k1, yo, k2tog, p1, ssk, yo, k1, yo, CDD, yo, k5, k2tog, yo, p1, k3.

Work repeats of Rows 9 - 21, until desired length is reached, or you're almost out of yarn.

Work Rows 1 - 6 once more. Bind off knitwise.

PATTERN WITH CHART

Using long tail method, cast on 35 sts. Rows 1 - 6: Knit.

Work repeats of Slowdive chart until desired length is reached, or you're almost out of yarn. Work Rows 1 - 6 once more. Bind off knitwise.

FINISHING

Weave in any ends, and wet block.

☐ RS: Knit WS: Purl

⊡ RS: Purl WS: Knit

◯ Yarn over

╱ K2tog

╲ Ssk

⋏ Cdd

⋏ K3tog

SLOWDIVE CHART

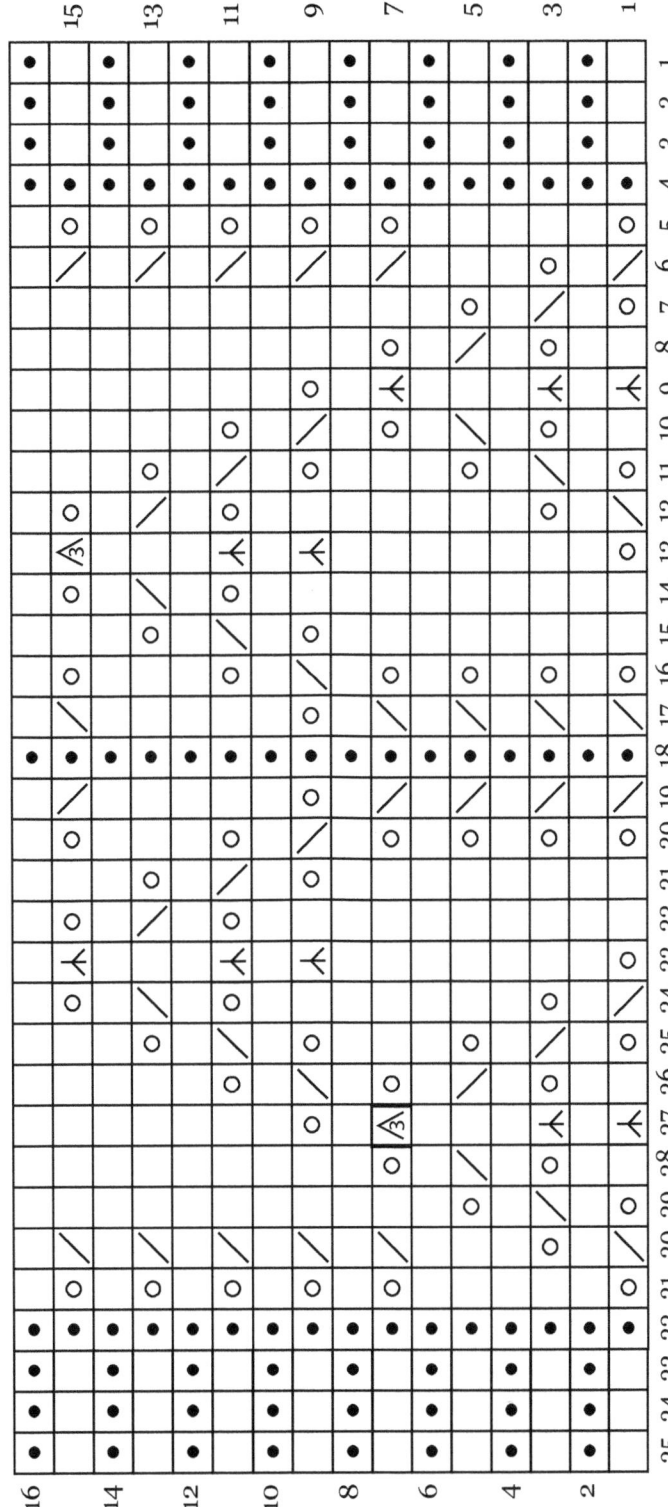

SPELLBOUND

Shetland lace worked in sections create this fascinating wide scarf. I love this deep purple color!

REQUIRED SKILLS

Intermediate knitting skills
Increases / decreases

MEASUREMENTS

Before blocking: 10 inches / 25.5 cm wide x 52 inches / 132 cm high

MATERIALS

Dragonfly Fibers Squishy Lace (100% Merino; 870 yds / 796 m per 113 g skein); color: Arya; 1 skeins, or approx. 400 yds / 365 m of laceweight yarn
US#5 / 3.75 mm needle
Large-eyed, blunt sewing needle

GAUGE

Before blocking: 40 sts x 40 rows = 4 inches / 10 cm in garter stitch

DESIGN NOTES

Added classic Shetland edging detail to the 27 st pattern, as well as adding top and bottom edging treatments.

PATTERN NOTES

Spellbound is worked in three sections; the lower lace panel, the middle (main) part of the scarf, and then an upper lace panel is worked and sewn on. To eliminate the upper and lower lace sections, cast on 51, and work Chart B, or the Middle Lace panel throughout.

PATTERN WITHOUT CHART

Lower lace
Using long tail method, cast ton 9 sts.

Row 1: K2, yo, k3, yo, ssk, k2.

Row 2 (and all even rows): K2, yo, ssk, k to end of row.

Row 3: K2, yo, k4, yo, ssk, k2.

Row 5: K2, yo, k5, yo, ssk, k2.

Row 7: K2, yo, k6, yo, ssk, k2.

Row 9: K2, yo, k7, yo, ssk, k2.

Row 11: K2, yo, k8, yo, ssk, k2.

Row 13: K2, yo, k9, yo, ssk, k2.

Row 15: Bind off 7, k5, yo, ssk, k2.

Work a further three repeats of Rows 1 - 16, then one repeat of Rows 1 - 15, binding off all but the last st on Row 15.

Turn your work so that the long flat edge of the lace is facing you, and pick up and knit 50 sts. 51 total sts. Purl 1 row, placing stitch markers after 9th and 42nd stitches.

Middle lace

Row 1: K2, yo, k3, yo, ssk, sm, k4, p1, yo, ssk, yo, k1, CDD, k1, yo, k2tog, yo, k2, yo, k2tog, p1, ssk, yo, k2, yo, ssk, yo, k1, CDD, k1, yo, k2tog, yo, p1, k4, sm, yo, ssk, k3, yo, k2.

Row 2 (and all even rows): K to 2 sts before marker, yo, ssk, sm, k4, p13, k1, p13, k4, sm, yo, ssk, k to end of row.

Row 3: K2, yo, k4, yo, ssk, sm, k4, p1, k1, yo, ssk, yo, CDD, yo, k2tog, yo, k3, yo, k2tog, p1, ssk, yo, k3, yo, ssk, yo, CDD, yo, k2tog, yo, k1, p1, k4, sm, yo, ssk, k4, yo, k2.

Row 5: K2, yo, k5, yo, ssk, sm, k4, p1, k2, yo, ssk, k1, k2tog, yo, k4, yo, k2tog, p1, ssk, yo, k4, yo, ssk, k1, k2tog, yo, k2, p1, k4, sm, yo, ssk, k5, yo, k2.

Row 7: K2, yo, k6, yo, ssk, sm, k4, p1, yo, ssk, k1, yo, CDD, yo, k5, yo, k2tog, p1, ssk, yo, k5, yo, k3tog, yo, k1, k2tog, yo, p1, k4, sm, yo, ssk, k6, yo, k2.

Row 9: K2, yo, k7, yo, ssk, sm, k4, p1, yo, ssk, k2, yo, ssk, yo, k1, CDD, k1, yo, k2tog, yo, p1, yo, ssk, yo, k1, CDD, k1, yo, k2tog, yo, k2, k2tog, yo, p1, k4, sm, yo, ssk, k7, yo, k2,

Row 11: K2, yo, k8, yo, ssk, sm, k4, p1, yo, ssk, k3, yo, ssk, yo, CDD, yo, k2tog, yo, k1, p1, k1, yo, ssk, yo, CDD, yo, k2tog, yo, k3, k2tog, yo, p1, k4, sm, yo, ssk, k8, yo, k2.

Row 13: K2, yo, k9, yo, ssk, sm, k4, p1, yo, ssk, k4, yo, ssk, k1, k2tog, yo, k2, p1, k2, yo, ssk, k1, k2tog, yo, k4, k2tog, yo, p1, k4, sm, yo, ssk, k9, yo, k2

Row 15: Bind off 7, k5, yo, ssk, sm, k4, p1, yo, ss, k5, yo, k3tog, yo, k1, yo, k2tog, p1, ssk, yo, k1, yo, CDD, yo, k5, k2tog, yo, p1, k4, sm, yo, ssk, k to end of row.

Row 16: Bind off 7 sts, p5, yo, ssk, sm, k5, p13, k1, p13, k5, sm, yo, k5.

Repeat Rows 1 - 16 until desired length is reached. Bind off. Break yarn.

Top Lace.

Using longtail method, cast on 9 sts.

Row 1: K2, yo, ssk, k3, yo, k2.

Row 2: K6, yo, ssk, k2.

Row 3: K2, yo, ssk, k4, yo, k2.

Row 4: K7, yo, ssk, k2.

Row 5: K2, yo, ssk, k5, yo, k2.

Row 6: K8, yo, ssk, k2.

Row 7: K2, yo, ssk, k6, yo, k2.

Row 8: K9, yo, ssk, k2.

Row 9: K2, yo, ssk, k7, yo, k2.

Row 10: K10, yo, ssk, k2.

Row 11: K2, yo, ssk, k8, yo, k2.

Row 12: K11, yo, ssk, k2.

Row 13: K2, yo, ssk, k9, yo, k2.

Row 14: K12, yo, ssk, k2.

Row 15: K2, yo, ssk, k to end of row.

Row 16: Bind off 7 sts, k5, yo, ssk, k2.

Work four more repeats of Rows 1 - 16, binding off all sts on Row 16 of the last repeat.

Lay the top lace along the bound off edge of Spellbound, and sew them together.

PATTERN WITH CHART

Lower Lace

Using longtail method, cast on 9 sts. Work Rows 1 - 16 of scarf 10 chart A a total of 5 times, binding off all sts on Row 15 of final repeat. Turn your work so that the long flat edge of the lace is facing you, and pick up and knit 50 sts. 51 total sts. Purl 1 row.

Middle lace

Work repeats of Scarf 10 chart B, until scarf is desired length. Bind off all sts of your final Row 16. Break yarn.

Top Lace

Using longtail method, cast on 9 sts. Work Rows 1 - 16 of of scarf 10 chart C a total of 5 times, binding off all sts on the final row. Lay the lace panel across the bound off edge of your scarf and sew them together.

FINISHING

Weave in any ends, and wet block.

LOWER LACE CHART

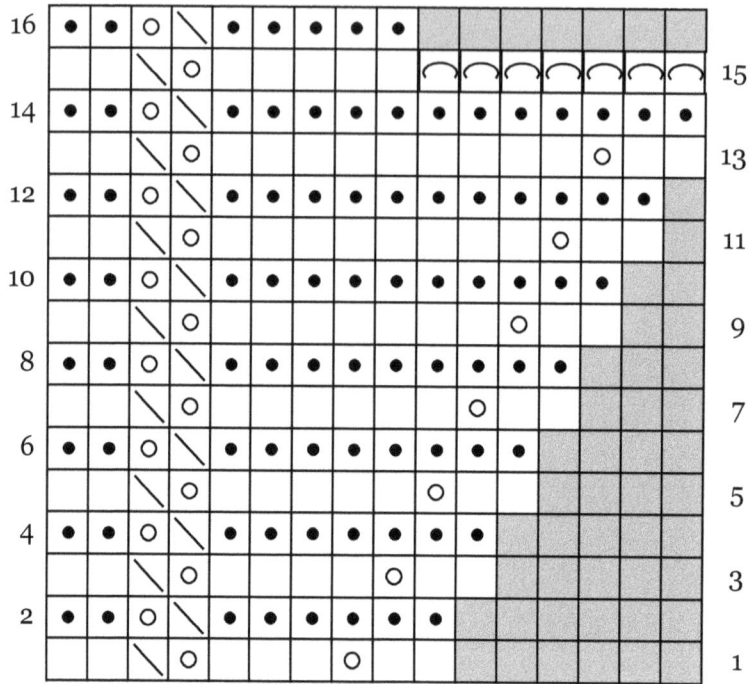

TOP LACE CHART

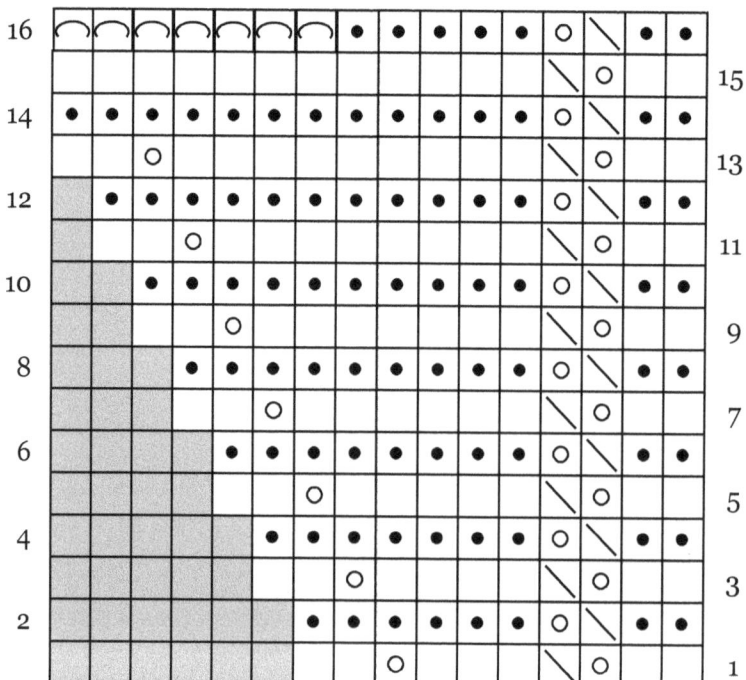

MIDDLE LACE CHART

PLAYGROUND TWIST

Nothing like a good set of cables to rev my knitting motor! This would be an excellent pattern to practice cabling without a cable needle.

REQUIRED SKILLS
Basic knitting skills
Simple cable sts

MEASUREMENTS
Before blocking: 5 inches / 12.75 cm wide x 80 inches / 203.25 cm high
After blocking: 5.5 inches / 14 cm wide x 82 inches / 208.25 cm high

MATERIALS
Unplanned Peacock Superwash Merino DK(100% Merino; 230 yds / 210 m per 100 g skein); color:C1: Indigo, C2: Dayglo; 1 skein of each, or approx 460 yds / 420 m of any DK weight yarn
US#8 / 5 mm needle
Cable needle
Large-eyed, blunt sewing needle

GAUGE
Before blocking: 32 sts x 24 rows = 4 inches / 10 cm in stitch pattern

DESIGN NOTES
Playground Twist is a repeated 40 st diamond cable pattern. To make this scarf wider, consider adding columns of the k2, p2 rib either side of the cable..

SPECIAL STITCHES
2/1 LpC - slip 2 sts to cn, hold in front, p1, k2 from cn
2/1 RpC - slip 1 st to cn, hold in back, k2, p1 from cn
2/2 LC - slip 2 sts to cn, hold in front, k2, k2 from cn
2/2 RC - slip 2 sts to cn, hold in back, k2, k2 from cn

PATTERN WITHOUT CHART

Using German Twisted, or your favorite stretchy method, cast on 40 sts.

Row 1: [P2, k2] four times, p2, k4, [p2, k2] four times, p2.

Row 2 (and all even rows): Work sts as they appear.
Repeat Rows 1 and 2 for 5 inches / 12.75 cm.

Row 3: [P2, k2] four times, p2, 2/2 LC, [p2, k2] four times, p2.

Row 5: [P2, k2] four times, p1, 2/1 RpC, 2/1 LpC, p1, [k2, p2] four times.

Row 7: [P2, k2] four times, 2/1 RpC, p2, 2/1 LpC, [k2, p2] four times.

Row 9: [P2, k2] three times, p2, 2/2 RC, p4, 2/2 LC, [p2, k2] three times, p2.

Row 11: [P2, k2] three times, p1, 2/1 RpC, 2/1 LpC, p2, 2/1 RpC, 2/1 LpC, p1, [k2, p2] three times.

Row 13: [P2, k2] three times, 2/1 RpC, p2, 2/1 LpC, 2/1 RpC, p2, 2/1 LpC, [k2, p2] three times.
Row 15: [P2, k2] twice, p2, [2/2 RC, p4] twice, 2/2 LC, p2, [k2, p2] twice.

Row 17: [P2, k2] twice, p1, [2/1 RpC, 2/1 LpC, p2] twice, 2/1 RpC, 2/1 LpC, p1, [k2, p2] twice.

Row 19: [P2, k2] twice, [2/1 RpC, p2, 2/1LpC] three times, [k2, p2] twice.

Row 21: P2, k2, p2, 2/2 RC, [p4, 2/2 LC] three times, p2, k2, p2.

Row 23: P2, k2, p1, [2/1 RpC, 2/1 LpC, p2] three times, 2/1 RpC, 2/1 LpC, p1, k2, p2.

Row 25: P2, k2, [2/1 RpC, p2, 2/1 LpC] four times, k2, p2.

Row 27: P2, [2/2 RC, p4] 4 times, 2/2 LC, p2.

Row 29: P2, [k4, p4] four times, k4, p2.

Row 31: P2, 2/2 LC, [p4, 2/2 RC] four times, p2.

Row 33: P2, k2, [2/1 LpC, p2, 2/1 RpC] four times, k2, p2.

Row 35: P2, k2, p1, [2/1 LpC, 2/1 RpC, p2] three times, 2/1 LpC, 2/1 RpC, p1, k2, p2.

Row 37: P2, k2, p2, [2/2 LC, p4] three times, 2/2 RC, p2, k2, p2.

Row 39: [P2, k2] twice, [2/1 LpC, p2, 2/1 RpC] three times, [k2, p2] twice.

Row 41: [P2, k2] twice, p1, [2/1 LpC, 2/1 RpC, p2] twice, 2/1 LpC, 2/1 RpC, p1, [k2, p2] twice.
Row 43: [P2, k2] twice, p2, 2/2 LC, [p4, 2/2 RC] twice, p2, [k2, p2] twice.

Row 45: [P2, k2] three times, [2/1 LpC, p2, 2/1 RpC] twice, [k2, p2] three times.

Row 47: [P2, k2] three times, p1, 2/1 LpC, 2/1 RpC, p2, 2/1 LpC, 2/1 RpC, p1, [k2, p2] three times.

Row 49: [P2, k2] three times, p2, 2/2

LC, p4, 2/2 RC, p2, [k2, p2] three times.

Row 51: [P2, k2] four times, 2/1 LpC, p2, 2/1 RpC, [k2, p2] four times.

Row 53: [P2, k2] four times, p1, 2/1 LpC, 2/1 RpC, p1, [k2, p2] four times.

Row 55: [P2, k2] four times, p2, 2/2 LC, p2, [k2, p2] four times.

Row 56: Work sts as they appear.

If working the scarf in two colors, repeat Rows 1 - 56, twice more, switch colors, working an initial purl only row on the WS to switch, then work three full repeats of Rows 1 - 56, then work repeats of Rows 1 and 2 for five inches / 12.75 cm. Bind off in pattern.

If working the scarf in one color, repeat Rows 1 - 56 six times, then work repeats of Rows 1 and 2 for five inches / 12.75 cm. Bind off in pattern.

PATTERN WITH CHART

Using German Twisted, or your favorite stretchy method, cast on 40 sts.

Work repeats of Playground Twist chart Rows 1 and 2 for 5 inches / 12.75 cm.

If working the scarf in two colors, work repeats of Rows 1 - 56 three times, changing color by working the third repeat of Row 56 by purling the entire row in the new color. Work three further repeats of Rows 1 - 15, then repeats of Rows 1 and 2 for 5 inches / 12.75 cm. Bind off in pattern.

FINISHING

Weave in any ends, and wet block.

☐ RS: Knit WS: Purl

⊡ RS: Purl WS: Knit

▱ 2/1 LpC

▱ 2/1 RpC

▱ 2/2 LC

▱ 2/2 RC

STARGAZER

Ok, I admit it—this scarf was inspired by the demigorgon monster in Stranger Things. I started out with a diamond shape and went from there.

DESIGN NOTES

I took away the rib columns from Playground Twist, leaving only the central diamond shape, joining nine of these diamonds together to form a collar.

REQUIRED SKILLS

Advanced knitting skills
Cables
Intermediate increases / decreases

MEASUREMENTS

Before blocking: 23 inches / 58.5 cm neck edge x 7.5 inches / 19 cm high
After blocking: 23 inches / 58.5 cm neck edge x 7.5 inches / 19 cm high

MATERIALS

Deep Dyed Yarns Align (80% Merino, 20% Nylon; 320 yds / 293 m per 100g kein); color: Coraline; 1 skein, or approx. 320 yds / 293 m of any fingering weight yarn
US#4 / 3.5 mm needle
Cable needle
8 stitch markers
Large-eyed, blunt sewing needle

GAUGE

Before blocking: 32 sts x 32 rows = 4 inches / 10 cm in stitch pattern

SPECIAL STITCHES

M1 - pick up the bar between the next 2 sts and purl it
P2togtbl - p2sts together through the back loop
2/1 LpC - slip 2 sts to cn, hold in front, p1, k2 from cn
2/1 RpC - slip 1 st to cn, hold in back, k2, p1 from cn
2/2 LC - slip 2 sts to cn, hold in front, k2, k2 from cn
2/2 RC - slip 2 sts to cn, hold in back, k2, k2 from cn
2/2 RpCdec - slip 2 sts to cn, hold in back, k2, p2tog from cn
2/2 LpCdec - slip 2 sts to cn, hold in front, p2tog, k2 from cn

PATTERN NOTES

If adding wedges, please note that you'll need around 40 yds of yarn per wedge.

PATTERN WITHOUT CHART

Using German Twisted, or your favorite stretchy method, cast on 144 sts, placing a stitch maker after every 16th stitch.

Row 1: *P2, k2, p2, k4, p2, k2, p2; repeat from * to end of row.

Row 2 (and all even rows, unless otherwise stated): Work sts as they appear.

Row 3: *P2, k2, M1, p2, 2/2 LC, p2, M1, k2, p2; repeat from * to end of row.

Row 5: *P2, k2, M1, p3, k4, p3, M1, k2, p2; repeat from * to end of row.

Row 7: *P2, k2, M1, p4, 2/2 LC, p4, M1, p2, k2; repeat from * to end of row.

Row 9: *P2, k2, M1, p4, 2/1 RpC, 2/1 LpC, p4, M1, k2, p2; repeat from * to end of row.

Row 11: *P2, k2, M1, p4, 2/1 RpC, p2, 2/1 LpC, p4, M1, k2, p2; repeat from * to end of row.

Row 13: *P2, k2, M1, p3, 2/2 RC, p4, 2/2 LC, p3, M1, k2, p2; repeat from * to end of row.

Row 15: *P2, k2, M1, p3, 2/1, RpC, 2/1 LpC, p2, 2/1 RpC, 2/1 LpC, p3, M1, k2, p2; repeat from * to end of row.

Row 17: *P2, k2, M1, p3, 2/1 RpC, p2, 2/1 LpC, p2, 2/1 RpC, p2, 2/1 LpC, p3, M1, k2, p2; repeat from * to end of row.

Row 19: *P2, k2, M1, p2, 2/2 RC, [p4, 2/2 LC] twice, p2, M1, k2, p2; repeat from * to end of row.

Row 21: *P2, k2, M1, [p2, 2/1 RpC, 2/1 LpC] three times, p2, M1, k2, p2; repeat from * to end of row.

Row 23: *P2, k2, M1, p2, [2/1 RpC, p2, 2/1 LpC] three times, p2, M1, k2, p2; repeat from * to end of row.

Row 25: *P2, k2, p2, [2/2 RC, p4] three times, 2/2 LC, p2, k2, p2; repeat from * to end of row.

Row 27: *P2, k2, p1, [2/1 RpC, 2/1 LpC, p2] three times, 2/1 RpC, 2/1 LpC, p1, k2, p2; repeat from * to end of row

Row 29: *P2, k2, [2/1 RpC, p2, 2/1 LpC] four times, k2, p2; repeat from * to end of row.

Row 31: *P2, k2, 2/2 RC, [p4, 2/2 LC] four times, p2; repeat from * to end of row.

Row 33: *P2, [k4, p4] 4 times, k2, p2; repeat from * to end of row.

Row 35: *P2, [2/2 LC, p4] four times, 2/2 RC, p2; repeat from * to end of row.

Row 37: *P2, k2, [2/1 LpC, p2, 2/1 RpC] four times, k2, p2; repeat from * to end of row.

Row 39: *P2, k2, p1, [2/1 LpC, 2/1 RpC, p2] three times, 2/1 LpC, 2/1 RpC, p1, k2, p2; repeat from * to end of row.

From this point on, you'll be working back and forth on each wedge individually.

Row 41: P2, k2, p2, 2/2 LpCdec, [p4, 2/2 LC] twice, p4, 2/2 RpCdec, p2, k2, p2. 34 sts.

Row 43: P2, k2, p2togtbl, p1, [2/1 LpC, p2, 2/1 RpC] three times, p1, p2tog, k2, p2.

Row 45: P2, k2, p2togtbl, p1, [2/1 LpC, 2/1 RpC, p2] twice, 2/1 LpC, 2/1 RpC, p1, p2tog, k2, p2.

Row 47: P2, k2, p2togtbl, p1, 2/1 LpCdec, p4, 2/2 RC, p4, 2/1 RpCdec, p1, p2tog, k2, p2.

Row 49: P2, k2, p2togtbl, p1, [2/1 LpC, p2, 2/1 RpC] twice, p1, p2tog, k2, p2.

Row 51: P2, k2, p2togtbl, p1, 2/1 LpC, 2/1 RpC, p2, 2/1 LpC, 2/1 RpC, p1, p2tog, k2, p2.

Row 53: P2, k2, p2togtbl, p1, 2/1 LpCdec, p4, 2/1 RpCdec, p1, p2tog, k2, p2.

Row 55: P2, k2, p2togtbl, p1, 2/1LpC, p2, 2/1 RpC, p1, p2tog, k2, p2.

Row 57: P2, k2, p2togtbl, 2/1 LpC, 2/1 RpC, p1, p2tog, k2, p2.

Row 59: P2, k2, p2togtbl, p1, 2/2 LC, p1, p2tog, k2, p2.

Row 61: P2, k2, p1, ssk, k2tog, p1, k2, p2.

Row 63: P2, k2, p2togtbl, p2tog, k2, p2. 10 sts.

Row 64: K2, p2, k2, p2, k2.

Bind off in pattern. Break yarn.
Work Rows 41 - 64 for each individual wedge.

PATTERN WITH CHART

Using German Twisted, or your favorite stretchy method, cast on 144 sts, placing a stitch maker after every 16th stitch.

Work Rows 1 - 40 across each row, using the stitch markers to help denote where each wedge is.

Rows 41 - 64: Work across one wedge only.

Bind off after Row 64, and join yarn to work Row 41 of next wedge.
Repeat for each remaining wedge.

FINISHING

Weave in any ends, and wet block.

	No stitch
	RS: Knit WS: Purl
•	RS: Purl WS: Knit
M	Make 1
/	K2tog
\	Ssk
•/	P2tog
•≠	P2togtbl
	2/1 LpC
	2/1 RpC
	2/2 LC
	2/2 RC
	2/2 RpCdec
	2/2 LpCdec

ABBREVIATIONS

- *2/1 LpC* - slip 2 sts to cn, hold in front, p1, k2 from cn
- *2/1 RpC* - slip 1 st to cn, hold in back, k2, p1 from cn
- *2/2 LC* - slip 2 sts to cn, hold in front, k2, k2 from cn
- *2/2 RC* - slip 2 sts to cn, hold in back, k2, k2 from cn
- *2/2 RpCdec* - slip 2 sts to cn, hold in back, k2, p2tog from cn
- *2/2 LpCdec* - slip 2 sts to cn, hold in front, p2tog, k2 from cn
- *CDD* - central double decrease, slip 1 knitwise, k2tog, pass slipped st over
- *cn* - cable needle
- *k* - knit
- *k2tog* - knit 2 sts together
- *k3tog* - knit 3 sts together
- *p* - purl
- *p2tog* - purl 2 sts together
- *p2togtbl* - purl 2 sts together through the back loop
- *pm* - place marker
- *rm* - remove marker
- *rm* - slip marker
- *rnd(s)* - round(s)
- *ssk* - slip first st knitwise, slip second st purlwise, knit them together
- *st(s)* - stitch(es)
- *wyib* - with yarn in back of work
- *wyif* - with yarn in front of work
- *yo* - yarn over

CREDITS

Even though this book has my name on the cover, as always, these collections are a collaboration between many people, to whom I give heartfelt thanks!

Firstly, thanks go out to Shannon, for words and things and stuff. You are the BEST!

To my sample knitters, Amy, April, Erica and Rebecca! Your attention to detail and speedy needles are much appreciated.

I've been lucky enough in my career to work almost exclusively with indie dyers. I'm passionate about supporting these small businesses, who provide the stunning yarns, inspiration, and support. Your encouragement and friendship means the world! Thank you!

Alchemy Yarns of Transformation	http://www.alchemyyarns.com
Anzula	https://anzula.com
Deep Dyed Yarns	https://www.deepdyedyarns.com
Dragonfly Fibers	https://www.dragonflyfibers.com
Malabrigo Yarns	http://www.malabrigoyarn.com
Neighborhood Fiber Co.	https://neighborhoodfiberco.com
Ross Farm	https://www.therossfarm.com
Spunky Eclectic Yarns	https://www.spunkyeclectic.com
Unplanned Peacock Studio	https://www.unplannedpeacock.com
Youghiogheny Yarns	https://www.youghioghenyyarns.com

ABOUT ANDI

Andi Smith is a fifty-something designer, originally from England, now living in Ohio, USA. Andi is lucky enough to work as a tech editor, designer, and teacher.

Her books, *Big Foot Knits* and *Color Cables* are available from Cooperative Press (cooperativepress.com) and her first color cable collection, Synchronicity, is available digitally on Ravelry:

https://www.ravelry.com/patterns/sources/synchronicity/patterns

Andi can be found on

- Facebook: https://www.facebook.com/andismithdesigns
- Instagram: https://www.instagram.com/iamknitbrit
- Ravelry: https://www.ravelry.com/people/knitbrit

ABOUT CP

Cooperative Press was founded in 2007 by Shannon Okey, a voracious reader as well as writer and editor, who had been doing freelance acquisitions work, introducing authors with projects she believed in to editors at various publishers.

Although working with traditional publishers can be very rewarding, there are some books that fly under their radar. They're too avant–garde, or the marketing department doesn't know how to sell them, or they don't think they'll sell 50,000 copies in a year.

5,000 or 50,000. Does the book matter to that 5,000? Then it should be published.

In 2009, Cooperative Press (cooperativepress. com) changed its name to reflect the relationships we have developed with authors working on books. We work together to put out the best quality books we can and share in the proceeds accordingly.

Thank you for supporting independent publishers and authors.

Cooperative Press can be found on

- Facebook: http://www.facebook.com/cooperativepress
- Instagram: http://www.instagram.com/cooperativepress
- Ravelry: http://www.ravelry.com/people/cooperativepress
- Web/shop: http://cooperativepress.com

www.ingramcontent.com/pod-product-compliance
Lightning Source LLC
Chambersburg PA
CBHW042134160426
43199CB00021B/2906